Spring Harvest
Bible Workbook

MATTHEW

Sermon on the Mount

Authentic

MILTON KEYNES · COLORADO SPRINGS · HYDERABAD

SPRING HARVEST

Equipping the Church for action

Copyright © 2001 Jenny Baker

First published in 2001 by Spring Harvest Publishing Division
and Paternoster Lifestyle

Reprinted 2004, 2005, 2006, 2007, 2008

14 13 12 11 10 09 08   12 11 10 9 8 7 6

Authentic Media, 9 Holdom Avenue, Bletchley, Milton Keynes, Bucks., MK1 1QR
1820 Jet Stream Drive, Colorado Springs, CO 80921, USA
Medchal Road, Jeedimetla Village, Secunderabad 500 055, A.P., India
www.authenticmedia.co.uk

Authentic Media is a division of IBS-STL U.K., limited by guarantee, with its Registered
Office at Kingstown Broadway, Carlisle, Cumbria CA3 OHA. Registered in England &
Wales No. 1216232. Registered charity 270162.

*The 'set the scene' activity in Session Three is based on an idea
from Mission and Young People at Risk by Frontier Youth Trust,
available on CD, and is used by permission. For more information,
contact 0207 387 7165.*

British Library Cataloguing in Publication Data

A catalogue record for this book is available from the British Library

ISBN 978-1-85078-407-4

Designed by Chris Gander

Printed in Great Britain by Bell and Bain, Glasgow

CONTENTS

ABOUT THIS BOOK

The aim of this book is simple, to help you to study the Sermon on the Mount and to apply it to your life. Jesus commended those who heard his words and put them into practice. So expect to see changes in your life as a result of studying this amazing and challenging passage.

This book is written primarily for a group situation, but can easily be used by individuals who want to study the Sermon. It can be used in a variety of contexts, so it is perhaps helpful to spell out the assumptions that we have made about the groups that will use it. These can have a variety of names – homegroups, Bible study groups, cell groups – we've used housegroup as the generic term!

- The emphasis of the studies will be on the application of the Bible. Group members will not just learn facts, but will be encouraged to think 'How does this apply to me? What change does it require of me? What incidents or situations in my life is this relevant to?'

- Housegroups can encourage honesty and make space for questions and doubts. The aim of the studies is not to find the 'right answer', but to help members understand the Bible by working through their questions. The Christian faith often throws up paradoxes. Events in people's lives may make particular verses difficult to understand or believe. The housegroup should be a safe place to express these concerns.

- Housegroups can give opportunities for deep friendships to develop. Group members will be encouraged to talk about their experiences, feelings, questions, hopes and fears. They will be able to offer one another pastoral support and to get involved in each others' lives.

- There is a difference between being a collection of individuals who happen to meet together every Wednesday and being an effective group who bounce ideas off each other, spark inspiration and creativity, pooling their talents and resources to create solutions together: one whose whole is definitely greater than the sum of its parts. The process of working through these studies will encourage healthy group dynamics.

Space is given for you to write answers, comments, questions and thoughts. This book will not tell you what to think, but will help you to discover the truth of God's word through thinking, discussing, praying and listening.

FOR GROUP MEMBERS

- You will probably get more out of the study if you spend some time during the week reading the passage and thinking about the questions. Make a note of anything you don't understand.

- Pray that God will help you to understand the passage and show you how to apply it. Pray for other members in your group too, that they will find the study helpful.

- Be willing to take part in the discussions. The leader of the group is not there as the expert with all the answers. They will want everyone to get involved and to share their thoughts and opinions.

- However, don't dominate the group! If you are aware that you are saying a lot, make space for others to contribute. Be sensitive to other group members and aim to be encouraging. If you disagree with someone, say so but without putting down their contribution.

FOR INDIVIDUALS

- Although this book is written with a group in mind, it can also be easily used by individuals. You obviously won't be able to do the group activities suggested, but you can consider how you would answer the questions and write your thoughts in the space provided.

- You may find it helpful to talk to a prayer partner about what you have learned, and ask them to pray for you as you try to apply the Sermon on the Mount to your life.

- The New International Version of the text is printed in the book. If you usually use a different version, then read from your own Bible as well.

INTRODUCTION TO THE SERMON ON THE MOUNT

Early in his ministry Jesus climbed a hillside near Capernaum, followed by his disciples, who were eager to hear what he had to say. Since his baptism he had been dropping hints about the kingdom of heaven and his popularity had grown, helped by the miracles he performed. Now was the time to let everyone in on the secrets of his kingdom, presenting a radically different way of living that would lead to abundant life.

He spoke to an oppressed people living in an occupied country, longing desperately for a Messiah. First century Palestine was a place full of tension and pressure, inhabited by people who had very different religious and political beliefs, living side by side. Jesus spoke to them about an upside-down kingdom, where the poor in spirit are the ones who are blessed, not the religious leaders or the rich. He talked about a righteousness that had to go beyond that of the nit-picking Pharisees, and a loving heavenly Father who would provide all they needed. He presented them with a new set of priorities, and invited them to enter into his kingdom.

The Sermon on the Mount was never called a sermon by Jesus. It is possiby not a word-for-word record, but a summary of the teaching he gave, perhaps over a few days. Even two thousand years later, it retains its power to deeply challenge those who read it and answers the central question of the third millennium – how should we live?

John Stott said that the Sermon on the Mount 'is probably the best known part of the teaching of Jesus... arguably it is the least understood and certainly it is the least obeyed.' This will not be a comfortable read. These studies will help you understand more about this incredible passage. Whether they change your life or not will be up to you.

OTHER SPRING HARVEST PUBLICATIONS

SERMON ON THE MOUNT by Don Carson – £4.99

HUMANIFESTO – A rough guide to the Sermon on the Mount by Gerard Kelly – £4.99

SPRING HARVEST BIBLE STUDIES
(Workbook on Sermon on the Mount) by Jenny Baker – £2.50

(All available post-free from Spring Harvest, 14 Horsted Square, Uckfield, East Sussex, TN22 1QG. Tel. 01825 769000)

HOW SHOULD WE LIVE?

AIM: to get an overview of the Sermon on the Mount

Standing on a hillside in first century Palestine, Jesus announced to those eager to hear that a new kingdom was breaking into their lives. This manifesto of Jesus answers a question that has echoed throughout human history – how should we live?

TO SET THE SCENE
Think about who taught you to do the following activities: how to tie shoelaces, how to bake a cake, how to swim, how to pray.

Then think about what or who influenced the following decisions: what football team to support, where to live, what job to do, which church to go to.

Who are the teachers, both formal and informal, who have had the most impact on you?

1 Read the whole of the Sermon on the Mount. As you listen, write down:

• One thing you are glad to hear

• One thing that sounds challenging

• One thing you want to learn more about

How would you summarise the Sermon? Is it possible to condense it into a phrase?

2 Explore the diversity of the members of your housegroup.

For example, discuss where each person was born, the different jobs they have had, their ambitions and the personal achievements they are most proud of.

First century Palestine was an occupied country with people who held a wide range of political and religious beliefs. These words of Jesus spoke into the lives of all of them, and speak to all of us, calling us to a radically new way of life.

We will look at two major themes of the Sermon on the Mount.

3 One central theme of Jesus' teaching was the **kingdom of heaven**. It is mentioned fifty times in Matthew alone, eight of them in this Sermon.

set bounded area, Ruler, Rules, Ambassadors, Loyal subjects.

Brainstorm what you know about kingdoms.

4 How would you define the kingdom of heaven?

WHAT DOES
THE BIBLE SAY?

5 Look up these verses to discover when the kingdom will come:

Matthew 4:17; Matthew 12:28; Luke 22:18.

The kingdom of heaven is both now, and not yet. It is here, amongst us, but not yet complete! How would you explain this to a member of the church youth group?

Another major theme of the Sermon was a need to **live a very different lifestyle.**

WHAT DOES **SEARCH** THE BIBLE SAY?

6 Some would say that Matthew 6:8 is a good summary of the whole Sermon – 'Do not be like them'. Jesus calls us to a very different way of life to those outside the kingdom.

Who are we to be different from? Matthew 5:20; Matthew 6:7,32; Matthew 6:5,16.

Pharisees
Pagans
hypocrites.

7 From a quick glance through, what issues does the Sermon address?

We will see examples of this distinctive lifestyle over the next few weeks.

HOW DOES THIS APPLY TO ME

8 Write down all the different areas of your life – think of the groups you belong to, activities you do – both work and leisure; responsibilities you have; relationships that define you.

9 Christians have tended to separate their lives into two compartments: the sacred - activities such as church and prayer that we believe God is interested in, and the secular - activities such as work, going to the cinema, gardening, that we do the rest of the week. In this view, which of these areas would be counted as more spiritual, and which would be more worldly?

10 Jesus the King wants to rule over every part of our lives. The Sermon on the Mount doesn't just address spiritual things, but practical issues that we face every day – something for each of these areas of your life.

HOW DOES THIS APPLY TO ME Give a star rating to each part of your life according to how much the rule of the King is evident at the moment – ranging from one star for 'could do a lot better' to five stars for 'doing pretty well.'

WORSHIP

Hand out notepaper and envelopes. Ask everyone to write a letter to God at the start of this study. The letter could talk about their feelings, expectations, concerns and hopes, as they look forward to the detailed study of the Sermon on the Mount. It could be a prayer to ask God to come and rule over every part of their lives. It could include some of the questions to which they hope to find answers. Finish with a time of prayer together.

FOR NEXT WEEK

We will be looking at the Beatitudes – the type of people that Jesus calls blessed. During the week make a note of those individuals who are considered to be successful in society. Who is celebrated and looked up to? Who is deemed to have 'got it made'?

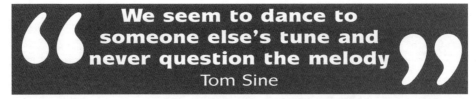

> **We seem to dance to someone else's tune and never question the melody**
> Tom Sine

CITIZENS OF THE KINGDOM

**AIM: to consider the kind of people that
Jesus calls blessed**

A quick flick through any magazine, or a few minutes of a TV chat show will show you the kind of people that our society celebrates. Jesus is not taken in by celebrity, wealth or power and stuns his listeners by describing the character of those who are blessed in his kingdom.

> *Now when he saw the crowds, he went up on a mountainside
> and sat down. His disciples came to him, and he began to teach them,
> saying:*
> *'Blessed are the poor in spirit, for theirs is the kingdom of heaven.*
> *Blessed are those who mourn, for they will be comforted.*
> *Blessed are the meek, for they will inherit the earth.*
> *Blessed are those who hunger and thirst for righteousness, for they will
> be filled.*
> *Blessed are the merciful, for they will be shown mercy.*
> *Blessed are the pure in heart, for they will see God.*
> *Blessed are the peacemakers, for they will be called sons of God.*
> *Blessed are those who are persecuted because of righteousness, for
> theirs is the kingdom of heaven.*
>
> *Blessed are you when people insult you, persecute you and falsely say
> all kinds of evil against you because of me. Rejoice and be glad,
> because great is your reward in heaven, for in the same way they
> persecuted the prophets who were before you.'*

Matthew 5:1-12

ENGAGING WITH
THE WORLD

TO SET THE SCENE
Look at the different publications available. In twos, using these and your own thoughts, make a list of the type of people who are considered blessed in society today. Report back to the rest of the group.

READ MATTHEW 5:1-12

1 The Beatitudes describe the qualities you would expect to find in a follower of Christ. Compare them to the list you have just made.

ENGAGING WITH
THE WORLD

2 Rewrite the Beatitudes to reflect the beliefs of today's society. In twos, write three 'Blessed are' statements – perhaps thinking about what kind of person is valued, what kind of action is valued and what is done to those who are considered blessed. Gather together the group's contributions. What contrasts between their statements and Matthew 5 are most striking?

Look at the Beatitudes in more detail. What do they mean in practice? You can either work through questions 3 to 8, or do the case study on page 16.

WHAT DOES
SEARCH
THE BIBLE SAY?

3 Look at the first three statements – the Bible reference gives an example of someone who displays that characteristic. What does it mean to:

- Verse 3: be poor in spirit? (Luke 18:13)

- Verse 4: mourn? (Matthew 26:75)

- Verse 5: be meek? (John 13:5)

What is the connection between the first half of the verse and the second? Why do the poor in spirit receive the kingdom of heaven? Who gives it to them? When do they receive it?

> Blessed is a very Christian word. Similar words or phrases used by those outside the church include: lucky, happy, successful, celebrated, those who have made it.

4 Verse 6: when do we usually get physically hungry and thirsty? What kind of experience causes a spiritual hunger and thirst for righteousness?

5 Verse 7: think of a situation or tell a story about someone who shows mercy to explain what it means.

Jesus says here that God will treat us in the way we treat others. Why? Can you think of other examples of this principle that Jesus gives in the gospels?

6 Verse 8: how can you tell if someone is pure in heart? How do you become pure in heart?

7 Verse 9: some may try to keep the peace by smoothing over and ignoring any disagreements. What is the difference between this and being a peacemaker?

Two children are arguing over what TV programme to watch. How might a peacekeeper and a peacemaker deal with this differently?

8 Verses 10 and 11: has this ever happened to you? Did you feel blessed at the time?! Why does being a Beatitude person provoke a negative reaction from the world?

HOW DOES THIS

APPLY TO ME

9 These are challenging characteristics to measure ourselves against! Write down a word that sums up how you feel when you read these verses. Which of these characteristics can be improved by your actions? Which require God to work in you?

ENGAGING WITH

THE WORLD

10 How realistic is it to try and live like this today? Won't you just get trampled on?

WORSHIP

Play a suitable piece of music in the background. Ask everyone to sit comfortably and close their eyes, with their hands in their laps, palms facing downwards. Read the Beatitudes slowly. Suggest they use this opportunity to confess to God where they don't display those characteristics. After a pause, ask them to turn their hands over, palms facing upwards, ready to receive. Read the Beatitudes once more and this time suggest people ask God to work in their lives in these areas. Finish with a prayer.

IN THE WEEK

Look out for examples of those who display characteristics of the Beatitudes. They might be members of your family or people in the news, church members, work colleagues or individuals from history. Make a note of them and bring it next week.

ACTIVITY PAGE

CASE STUDY

Alison is the headmistress of a busy secondary school that has just had quite a negative Ofsted inspection. Many of the pupils at the school are disruptive and her staff are rather demoralised. Alison also plays in the church worship group and preaches occasionally. If Alison embodies the characteristics in the Beatitudes, how would you expect them to be demonstrated in the following situations?

a) Her personal prayer time after hearing about the Ofsted report.

b) A meeting with a pupil and his Dad: the boy is facing exclusion for fighting and being rude to a teacher. The father explains that things at home have been difficult since his wife left a few months before.

c) Talking to a friend, who admits that she feels very disillusioned with God. She assumes Alison rarely has that problem.

d) In a worship team meeting: the worship leader is a teacher in another school, and he suggests that one of Alison's sixth formers should lead worship at the next service as a one-off.

e) Overhearing a conversation at the school gate: a parent thinks Alison lacks authority and is too soft because she is a churchgoer.

How realistic are your answers? Would someone really behave like that? Look at the other Beatitudes that may not have come up in your discussions so far. How would they be displayed in real life?

Alternatively, discuss a soap character that is familiar to everyone. How would this person change if they were to meet with God and display all the characteristics of the Beatitudes?

"Which is the right way up? Who decides?"

THE CHURCH COMMUNITY

Aim: To consider what kind of community Jesus intended the church to be

Jesus didn't preach this Sermon to give his followers some new ideas to talk about. He wanted to establish a community to live out the truth – to model life as God intended it to be lived. This community is the church.

> 'You are the salt of the earth. But if the salt loses its saltiness, how can it be made salty again? It is no longer good for anything, except to be thrown out and trampled by men.
>
> You are the light of the world. A city on a hill cannot be hidden. Neither do people light a lamp and put it under a bowl. Instead they put it on its stand, and it gives light to everyone in the house. In the same way, let your light shine before men, that they may see your good deeds and praise your Father in heaven.
>
> Do not think that I have come to abolish the Law or the Prophets; I have not come to abolish them but to fulfil them. I tell you the truth, until heaven and earth disappear, not the smallest letter, not the least stroke of a pen, will by any means disappear from the Law until everything is accomplished. Anyone who breaks one of the least of these commandments and teaches others to do the same will be called least in the kingdom of heaven, but whoever practises and teaches these commands will be called great in the kingdom of heaven. For I tell you that unless your righteousness surpasses that of the Pharisees and the teachers of the law, you will certainly not enter the kingdom of heaven.'

Matthew 5:13-20

ENGAGING WITH THE WORLD

TO SET THE SCENE

Think about expressions of community in your local area. Where do people get together and for what reasons? What local groups do you belong to? Where do you find a sense of community?

Look at some pictures of groups of people and places. Which of these fit with your idea of community? Which provide fresh ideas of what community could be? Which don't fit at all with your understanding of community?

READ MATTHEW 5:13-20

1 Discuss some of the positives of church. What is the church for? How is the church distinctive from any other collective group? What led you to join your local church?

Jesus uses three metaphors to describe the essential nature of his kingdom community – salt, light and a city set on a hill.

2 Verse 13: brainstorm some uses of salt, both contemporary and from the past. What do these uses tell us about the role of the church in the local community? Does your church function in this way? – give examples.

3 Metaphors are never exact parallels. Are there any aspects of salt that you think are not appropriate to the church?

4 Verse 14: brainstorm different types of light, and the purposes light is used for. See if your view of the church can be enriched by thinking of parallels between these lights and the role of the church. Which type of light best sums up your understanding of the church?

WHAT DOES SEARCH THE BIBLE SAY?

5 Verse 14: is Jesus contradicting himself? In John 8:12 he says he is the light and yet here he tells his disciples that they are the light.

6 Verse 14: In what ways should the church be like a city set on a hill? Does it fulfil this role in society? Why or why not?

Having given his vision for the role of the church, Jesus then goes on to talk about specific, radical hallmarks of his kingdom community. This gets more personal! The church can only be a corporate expression of what we are individually.

WHAT DOES SEARCH THE BIBLE SAY?

7 Talk about some of the different aspects of the Old Testament (The Law and the Prophets). In what ways does Jesus fulfil them?

8 The Pharisees were renowned for being very pedantic about obeying the letter of the law. How can our righteousness surpass theirs? Doesn't this smack of 'salvation by works' – trying to get into the kingdom by being good?

In what ways should our righteousness be different to that of the Pharisees?

HOW DOES THIS

APPLY TO ME

9 Salt needs to be thoroughly mixed into the food it flavours or preserves. How involved are you in the local community? Or are you too busy with church activities?

Fill in the time sheet on page 22 to show how you spend a typical week. Use colours to shade time spent with family, friends, church members, by yourself and with those who are not Christians. Where do you meet people outside the church? Are you happy with how you spend your week?

HOW DOES THIS

APPLY TO ME

10 Verse 16: how can your lifestyle, both as an individual and as part of a church community, become more visible and so bring glory to God?

WORSHIP

Have some salted foods, such as pistachio nuts or crisps, and a lit candle with some unlit nightlights beside it. Play some background music and give everyone some space to reflect on the community brainstorm that was done at the start. As they taste the crisps and nuts, they should ask God where he is calling them to be involved and pray for opportunities to flavour the community around them. They can light a nightlight and pray for those for whom they would like to be a light. After this time for individual reflection, spend some time praying corporately for opportunities for your housegroup and church to be salt and light.

IN THE WEEK

Look out for salt! Each time you use it or taste it, ask God to give you an opening to be salt in your community. Come back next week ready to share your experiences.

ACTIVITY PAGE

A timesheet to accompany question 9

	Morning				Afternoon				Evening			
Sunday												
Monday												
Tuesday												
Wednesday												
Thursday												
Friday												
Saturday												

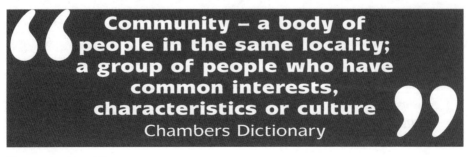

Community – a body of people in the same locality; a group of people who have common interests, characteristics or culture
Chambers Dictionary

Do you agree?

BEYOND THE LAW

AIM: to consider what 'righteousness that surpasses that of the Pharisees' looks like in practice

People have always tried to bridge the gap between themselves and God, but it just can't be done from our side. The Pharisees had taken the law given by God and turned it into a legalistic, pedantic and oppressive code. Jesus said that if we want to be righteous, we have to do better than that.

'You have heard that it was said to the people long ago, "Do not murder", and anyone who murders will be subject to judgement. But I tell you that anyone who is angry with his brother will be subject to judgement. Again, anyone who says to his brother, "Raca", is answerable to the Sanhedrin. But anyone who says "You fool!" will be in danger of the fire of hell.

Therefore, if you are offering your gift at the altar and there remember that your brother has something against you, leave your gift there in front of the altar. First go and be reconciled to your brother; then come and offer your gift.

Settle matters quickly with your adversary who is taking you to court. Do it while you are still with him on the way, or he may hand you over to the judge, and the judge may hand you over to the officer, and you may be thrown into prison. I tell you the truth, you will not get out until you have paid the last penny.

You have heard that it was said, "Do not commit adultery." But I tell you that anyone who looks at a woman lustfully has already committed adultery with her in his heart. If your right eye causes you to sin, gouge it out and throw it away. It is better for you to lose one part of your body than for your whole body to be thrown into hell. And if your right hand causes you to sin, cut it off and throw it away. It is better for you to lose one part of your body than for your whole body to go into hell.

It has been said "Anyone who divorces his wife must give her a certificate of divorce." But I tell you that anyone who divorces his wife, except for marital unfaithfulness, causes her to commit adultery and anyone who marries a woman so divorced commits adultery.

Again, you have heard that it was said to the people long ago, "Do not break your oath, but keep the oaths you have made to the Lord." But I tell you, Do not swear at all: either by heaven, for it is God's throne; or by earth, for it is his footstool; or by Jerusalem, for it is the city of the Great King. And do not swear by your head, for you cannot make even one hair white or black. Simply let your "Yes" be "Yes" and your "No", "No"; anything beyond this comes from the evil one.

You have heard that it was said "Eye for eye, and tooth for tooth." But I tell you, Do not resist an evil person. If someone strikes you on the right cheek, turn to him the other also. And if someone wants to sue you and take your tunic, let him have your cloak as well. If someone forces you to go one mile, go two miles. Give to the one who asks you, and do not turn away from the one who wants to borrow from you.

You have heard that it was said "Love your neighbour and hate your enemy." But I tell you: Love your enemies and pray for those who persecute you, that you may be sons of your Father in heaven. He causes his sun to rise on the evil and the good, and sends rain on the righteous and the unrighteous. If you love only those who love you, what reward will you get? Are not even the tax collectors doing that? And if you greet only your brothers, what are you doing more than others? Do not even pagans do that? Be perfect, therefore, as your heavenly Father is perfect.'

Matthew 5:21-48

TO SET THE SCENE

Now is a time for complete honesty and baring of souls – how many of you have broken the speed limit and so broken the law?! Did you justify it to yourself? What reasons did you use? What laws in this country would you like to see changed? Can you legislate for righteousness?

READ MATTHEW 5:21-48

WHAT DOES SEARCH THE BIBLE SAY?

1 What do each of these paragraphs have in common? (verses 21, 27, 31, 33, 38, 43).

Is Jesus criticising the law his Father had given?

Integrity of Temperament verses 21-26 and 38-48:

2 Is it wrong to be angry? In what circumstances have you felt your anger is justified? What type of anger does Jesus say is to be avoided?

3 Verses 38-42: what type of situations today might require this kind of reaction?

When does mistreatment become abuse that ought to be resisted?

Sexual Integrity verses 27-30:

4 Sexuality is a good gift from God. How has it been spoilt in our society?

How can we have a right attitude to our sexuality?

5 How does lust harm us?

Marital Integrity verses 31-32

Divorce is a very painful subject for many people. These are not the only words that Jesus spoke about it. (see Matthew 19:1-12).

6 What are some of the causes of marriage breakdown today?

How would Beatitude characteristics make a difference?

7 How can the church be salt and light in issues of marriage, cohabitation, divorce and remarriage?

Verbal integrity verses 33-37:

8 'We live in a world where dishonesty is epidemic.' Do you agree? Who do you trust to speak the truth?

How would you phrase these verses positively in one sentence?

9 What does kingdom righteousness look like in practice? Discuss some of the scenarios on page 28.

10 Christians are made righteousness by Jesus' death and resurrection. Why do we need to be concerned about our behaviour?

WORSHIP

Talking about God's standards of righteousness probably makes us very aware of how we have failed to live up to them. Have some bowls of warm water, soap and towels. Play some appropriate music in the background and invite people to confess their sins and weaknesses to God, especially in the areas you have considered: anger, sexuality, marriage and speech. They should take it in turns to wash their hands as they pray. Provide some hand cream, and invite everyone to put it on as they ask God to protect them by his Spirit and help them to be righteous. Use this prayer as a way of committing yourselves to integrity.

Leader: In our emotions, the way we deal with anger and in all our relationships

All: **Lord, we commit ourselves to kingdom integrity**.

L: In our sexuality, our thoughts and actions, and the way we treat one another

A: **Lord, we commit ourselves to kingdom integrity**.

L: In our marriage relationships, and in being salt and light to broken families

A: **Lord, we commit ourselves to kingdom integrity**.

L: In our speech, our promises, and in every way that we communicate

A: **Lord, we commit ourselves to kingdom integrity**.

Pass round pieces of seaside rock, if you can get hold of it. Rock has the name of the resort all the way through it. Likewise every part of our character needs to have kingdom integrity.

IN THE WEEK

Look out for those in the public eye who speak with integrity, or who stand by what they say. Bring newspaper cuttings along to the next session.

ACTIVITY PAGE

SCENARIOS

A woman who had suffered sexual and physical abuse for a number of years was told by a fellow Christian that she 'should not be angry, and should just forgive'. Is this good advice?

You are staying in a hotel overnight on business. The television in your room has access to lots of channels, including soft porn programmes. You feel tempted to watch – what would you do?

As you walk into church for the communion service, you see a parent who criticised you for letting her daughter stay up too late at a sleepover at your house last weekend. The situation has not been resolved and she hasn't spoken to you since. What do you do?

After reading Jesus' comments on lust and adultery, a teenager comments to you that once he's had a lustful thought, he might as well have sex, because Jesus is saying it's the same thing. What would you say?

Your neighbour borrowed your lawnmower and returned it damaged. She has now put a note through the door asking if she can borrow a stepladder to do some decorating. What do you do?

Your friend who is not a Christian has very colourful language! You are not so bothered about the effing and blinding, but you inwardly wince when he uses God's name as a swear word. What do you do?

> **Anybody can become angry – that is easy; but to be angry with the right person and to the right degree and at the right time, and for the right purpose and in the right way – that is not within everybody's power and is not easy**
> Aristotle (348-322BC)

KEEP IT SECRET

AIM

AIM: to consider the importance of secret spirituality – developing our relationship with God

We have looked at the radically different lifestyle that following Jesus requires. This week we will explore what that lifestyle is founded on – a real spirituality, a deep love for, and intimacy with, God.

> 'Be careful not to do your "acts of righteousness" before men, to be seen by them. If you do, you will have no reward from your Father in heaven. So when you give to the needy, do not announce it with trumpets, as the hypocrites do in the synagogues and on the streets, to be honoured by men. I tell you the truth, they have received their reward in full. But when you give to the needy, do not let your left hand know what your right hand is doing, so that your giving may be in secret. Then your Father, who sees what is done in secret, will reward you.
>
> But when you pray, do not be like the hypocrites, for they love to pray standing in the synagogues and on the street corners to be seen by men. I tell you the truth, they have received their reward in full. When you pray, go into your room, close the door and pray to your Father, who is unseen. Then your Father, who sees what is done in secret, will reward you. And when you pray, do not keep on babbling like pagans, for they think they will be heard because of their many words. Do not be like them, for your Father knows what you need before you ask him. This is how you should pray:
>
> Our Father in heaven,
> hallowed be your name,
> your kingdom come,
> your will be done
> on earth as it is in heaven.
> Give us today our daily bread.
> Forgive us our debts
> as we also have forgiven our debtors.
> And lead us not into temptation,
> but deliver us from the evil one.

For if you forgive men when they sin against you, your heavenly Father will also forgive you. But if you do not forgive men their sins, your Father will not forgive your sins.

When you fast, do not look sombre as the hypocrites do, for they disfigure their faces to show men they are fasting. I tell you the truth, they have received their reward in full. But when you fast, put oil on your head and wash your face, so that it will not be obvious to men that you are fasting, but only to your Father who is unseen, and your Father, who sees what is done in secret, will reward you.'

Matthew 6:1-18

TO SET THE SCENE

Play a game called 'When did you last...?' On strips of paper, write activities such as 'have a good laugh', 'cook a new recipe', 'read a good book'. People take it in turns to draw out an activity and talk about when they last did what is written on the paper. You are allowed to pass if you don't want to answer.

READ MATTHEW 6:1-18

WHAT DOES SEARCH THE BIBLE SAY?

1 There is a pattern to Jesus' words about giving, praying and fasting. Pick out the statements that he uses for all three.

What is the significance of Jesus saying 'when you give...' instead of 'if you give...?'

2 Why should these things be done in secret? After all, we've been looking at the importance of community.

3 Spirituality is a popular word these days – what does it mean?

How is the spirituality of kingdom people to be different to that of the Pharisees?

4 Christians need to know the truth about God, and to have a friendship with God. Although the two should be inseparable, sometimes Christians have emphasised one at the expense of the other. What is the danger of focusing too much on knowing the truth and having the right doctrine? What is the danger of overemphasising the need to experience God?

HOW DOES THIS

APPLY TO ME

5 Imagine a pendulum swinging between the two extremes above of experience and head knowledge – where on the pendulum swing are you? Or in which direction would you like to be moving?

6 Verse 1: how many ways might we complete this sentence: 'I'd love to give money to the poor but…'? How would you respond to that and encourage others to give?

7 Verse 5: when do you pray? Talk to each other about your experiences of prayer – not to show off like the Pharisees, but to discover how prayer fits into each others' lives.

8 Verse 16: fasting doesn't seem to be very common these days – why is that? Maybe everyone keeps it secret! Usually we go without food, but you can also fast from anything that you feel has too much prominence in your life, in order to devote time to God. What might those things be?

HOW DOES THIS

APPLY TO ME

9 Verse 9: Jesus gives us a model of prayer. In your experience, has the Lord's Prayer been a source of greater intimacy with God, or something that is repeated parrot-fashion?

10 Jesus talks about his Father rewarding our secret spirituality. Doesn't that contradict the idea of salvation by grace alone? What might that reward be?

WORSHIP

Give everyone an orange. Read the passage again, over background music if appropriate. Peel the orange, thinking about the superficial spirituality in your life that may need to be peeled away – doing things to impress others, wanting to live up to a certain image, lack of forgiveness, a self-centred faith. Pray as you peel, asking God to change your heart and enable you to develop a secret spirituality centred on him. Put the peelings in a rubbish bin to show those things are to be discarded, and enjoy the fruit! Continue to pray for one another.

FOR NEXT WEEK

Your task, should you choose to accept it, is to keep a record over the week of when you give, pray and fast. In the spirit of this session it will remain secret, but you may like to talk about what you discovered from this activity next week.

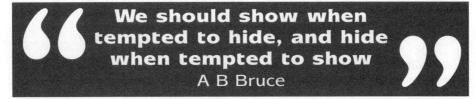

> **We should show when tempted to hide, and hide when tempted to show**
> A B Bruce

DO NOT WORRY

AIM: to consider the impact that kingdom priorities can have on our attitude to money

Money is rather a taboo subject in our society. We rarely discuss how much we earn, or how we spend our money, but Jesus had a lot to say about it in the gospels. Material wealth can easily be counterproductive to the values and impact of the kingdom. Jesus tells us to exchange our worry for trust in our Father.

'Do not store up for yourselves treasures on earth, where moth and rust destroy, and where thieves break in and steal. But store up for yourselves treasures in heaven, where moth and rust do not destroy, and where thieves do not break in and steal. For where your treasure is, there your heart will be also.

The eye is the lamp of the body. If your eyes are good, your whole body will be full of light. But if your eyes are bad, your whole body will be full of darkness. If then the light within you is darkness, how great is that darkness!

No-one can serve two masters. Either he will hate the one and love the other, or he will be devoted to the one and despise the other. You cannot serve both God and Money.

Therefore, I tell you, do not worry about your life, what you will eat or what you will drink; or about your body, what you will wear. Is not life more important than food and the body more important than clothes? Look at the birds of the air; they do not sow or reap or store away in barns and yet your heavenly Father feeds them. Are you not much more valuable than they? Who of you by worrying can add a single hour to his life?

And why do you worry about clothes? See how the lilies of the field grow. They do not labour or spin. Yet I tell you that not even Solomon in all his splendour was dressed like one of these. If that is how God clothes the grass of the field, which is here today and tomorrow is thrown into the fire, will he not much more clothe you, O you of little faith? So do not worry, saying, "What shall we eat?" or "What shall we drink?" or "What shall we wear?" For the pagans run after all these things, and your heavenly Father knows that you need them. But seek first his kingdom and his righteousness, and all these things will be given to you as well. Therefore do not worry about tomorrow, for tomorrow will worry about itself. Each day has enough trouble of its own.'

Matthew 6:19-34

TO SET THE SCENE
Brainstorm the different places that are now used for advertising. What is the most bizarre or annoying place that you have seen an advert? Look at some adverts from magazines or ones that have been videoed from the TV. What are they selling? What do they appeal to in order to make you buy the product? Does advertising have any affect on you?

READ MATTHEW 6:19-34

1 'Don't store up for yourselves treasures on earth.' Is Jesus saying it is wrong to be wealthy?

ENGAGING WITH

THE WORLD
2 Some say that shopping is the new religion. Think of parallels between shopping and religious activity. Do you agree with this statement? In what way can money rival God? (Verse 24)

3 How do you store up treasures in heaven?

4 Verse 24: do you own your possessions or do they own you? If a fire destroyed everything you owned, what would you be most upset about losing? Would you feel differently if you weren't fully insured?

5 Verse 25: Jesus tells us not to worry about food, drink or clothing. Do you tend to worry about these? What other things can be a source of worry?

6 We are told that aromatherapy candles and relaxation techniques will help to de-stress us. What does Jesus give as the reason not to worry (verses 25-33)?

WHAT DOES

SEARCH

THE BIBLE SAY?

7 Look back at the Lord's Prayer (verses 9-13). How can each phrase in the prayer help to allay our worries, especially about money?

8 The first request in the Lord's Prayer is for daily bread – what does this include? Discuss the essentials of life that you feel come into the category of daily bread, or do the activity on page 39 – giving financial advice to a new graduate.

ENGAGING WITH

THE WORLD

9 How would you explain the phrase 'Seek first the kingdom of God' to:

- someone in the Queen Vic?
- a member of the Royle Family?
- a work colleague or friend who is not a Christian?

10 Jesus promised that those who put the kingdom first would have all these things – food, drink, and clothes – given to them as well. Share stories of how this principle has worked in your life, or for others that you know.

WORSHIP

A meditation: hold some coins in your hand. Feel them; smell them; look closely at them.

What could this money buy – perhaps something to eat or something to read; something to entertain you, or a gift for a friend; a luxury or a necessity? How will you use it?

How do you feel about money? Does it cause worry, or bring blessing, or perhaps a bit of both?

Hear the words of Jesus: 'Do not store up for yourselves treasures on earth. Store up for yourselves treasures in heaven. Don't worry, saying "What shall we eat?" or "What shall we drink?" or "What shall we wear?" For the pagans run after all these things and your heavenly Father knows that you need them. Seek first his kingdom and his righteousness, and all these things will be given to you as well.'

Tell God about your worries. Thank him for his provision. Decide to trust him for your daily bread.

End with a time of prayer together.

FOR NEXT WEEK

During the week, look out for adverts and note the effect they have on you. Bring along the advert that you feel most contradicts the values of the kingdom.

ACTIVITY PAGE

Richard is a new graduate. He is about to start his first job as a pharmacist in a hospital in a new town. He has a reasonable amount of student debt to pay off, and will be renting a flat to begin with, although he would love to buy his own home as soon as possible.

As a Christian, Richard often prays 'Give us this day our daily bread', and understands this to mean that God will provide the essentials that he needs for his life. Which of the following do you think comes into the category of daily bread for Richard?

- Food and drink
- A house to live in
- Mobile phone
- Membership of the gym
- A girlfriend
- Money to give to charity
- Clothes to wear for work and leisure
- A holiday in the sun to recover from his first year at work
- Anything else that is not listed here?

- Money to repay his loan
- Nights out to unwind
- Trips to visit his family and friends
- CD player, TV and DVD player
- Car to drive to his workplace

Will this change when Richard is in his forties, with a better-paid job and a family to support?

What three top tips for having a right attitude to money would you give Richard, based on Matthew 6:19-34?

1

2

3

HOW DOES THIS

APPLY TO ME

Getting personal! What about you? How do you decide your priorities for spending and what your standard of living should be? Is this easier to do if you have more money or less? How should our awareness of life in the Two-Thirds World affect our spending? Do we let it?

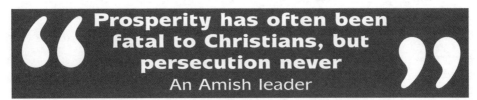

> **Prosperity has often been fatal to Christians, but persecution never**
> An Amish leader

FORGIVE AND BE FORGIVEN

AIM: to consider how our friendship with the King should affect our relationships with others

All the way through the Sermon on the Mount, Jesus shows how the values, beliefs and behaviour of his followers should be different to that of the world around them. Our relationships with others should be characterised by forgiveness. Our attitudes toward others must not be harshly critical and judgmental. A tall order? Not when we remember the friendship we have with God.

'Do not judge, or you too will be judged. For in the same way you judge others, you will be judged, and with the measure you use, it will be measured to you.

Why do you look at the speck of sawdust in your brother's eye and pay no attention to the plank in your own eye? How can you say to your brother, "Let me take the speck out of your eye", when all the time there is a plank in your own eye? You hypocrite, first take the plank out of your own eye, and then you will see clearly to remove the speck from your brother's eye.

Do not give dogs what is sacred; do not throw your pearls to pigs. If you do, they may trample them under their feet, and then turn and tear you to pieces.

Ask and it will be given to you; seek and you will find; knock and the door will be opened to you. For everyone who asks receives; he who seeks finds; and to him who knocks, the door will be opened.

Which of you, if his son asks for bread, will give him a stone? Or if he asks for a fish, will give him a snake? If you, then, though you are evil, know how to give good gifts to your children, how much more will your Father in heaven give good gifts to those who ask him! In everything, do to others what you would have them do to you, for this sums up the Law and the Prophets.'

Matthew 7:1-12

TO SET THE SCENE

The most popular response to crime seems to be 'let's get revenge', rather than 'let's forgive'. What is a kingdom response to people like Myra Hindley, Jon Venables and Robert Thompson? Parents have campaigned to stop paedophiles being housed near where they live – is that reaction justified? Is 'forgive and forget' a biblical concept?

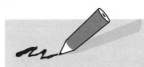

READ MATTHEW 7:1-12

1 What happens when we judge others?

2 Verse 1: 'Do not judge, or you will too will be judged' may be one of the most frequently misused quotations from the Bible. In what ways are Christians expected to judge and to use discernment? What kind of judgement does Jesus condemn?

3 Verse 1-5: we have looked at what it means to be righteous. How might self-righteousness lead to wrong judgement, and kingdom righteousness lead to right judgement?

4 Verse 6 has been used as an argument against evangelism – we shouldn't give the precious gospel to pagans who don't appreciate it! However, the context here is judging others. What is Jesus saying?

WHAT DOES SEARCH THE BIBLE SAY?

5 Look back at the verses immediately following the Lord's Prayer (6:14,15). We often talk about the unconditional nature of God's love; why does he make his forgiveness conditional?

6 What effect does unforgiveness have on us?

ENGAGING WITH THE WORLD

7 How would you encourage someone to forgive? Read the letter on page 44 and think how you would respond.

8 Verse 9: what kind of requests do children make of their parents? Think back to when you were a child, or about children that you know. How do parents feel about these requests?

9 Verse 7: Jesus encourages us to be persistent and confident in our relationship with God. What stops us asking, seeking and knocking? How do you cope with prayers that don't seem to be answered?

HOW DOES THIS APPLY TO ME?

10 What good gifts has your heavenly Father given you?

WORSHIP

Give everyone a piece of paper with an outline of a human person on it. Have lots of paints, crayons, pencils or felt pens available. Allow some space for people to think about where they need to forgive others, or where they need to ask God for harshly judgmental and critical. They should use appropriate colours to represent these thoughts on their outline as they pray to God about them. Murky greys and purples might be used to represent unforgiveness as a weight on someone's shoulders. Sharp jagged deep red shapes might represent judgmental feelings in someone's heart.

When everyone has finished their pictures, read Psalm 51:1-12. Leave space for them to pray out loud if they want to. Assure them of God's forgiveness by reading Psalm 103:10-18.

Hand out another outline and encourage everyone to use different colours to represent God's forgiveness, or how they would like to relate to others differently.

It can be hard to forgive. If anyone needs more space and time, encourage them to pray with a friend after the session.

FOR NEXT WEEK
As you watch TV, or see a film, or read the newspaper, think about how forgiveness would transform the situations in front of you.

ACTIVITY
Read the letter on page 44. From your understanding of God's forgiveness and the Sermon on the Mount, think about how you would respond to this lady. Write down some points that you would want to communicate if you were to have a conversation with her.

This is a very painful situation in which to forgive, but even minor incidents can arouse strong feelings. Would your advice differ if you were talking to a fellow Christian who was bearing a grudge against the churchwarden over the allocation of storage space in the church, and if so, how?

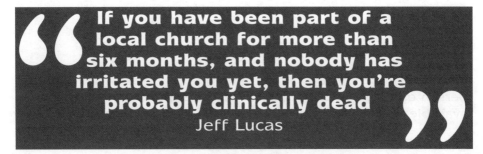

> **If you have been part of a local church for more than six months, and nobody has irritated you yet, then you're probably clinically dead**
> Jeff Lucas

ACTIVITY PAGE

Dear friend,

Four years ago my oldest son Matthew, who was six at the time, was killed in a car accident by a drunk driver. The bloke was well over the limit but only got charged with manslaughter and may well be out of prison next year. I am so angry that I'm afraid of what I might do to him if I saw him.

Why should he go free when I have to live with the pain of never seeing my son again? I want him to suffer like I am suffering. My two younger children were only three and one when Matthew died and they can hardly remember him. Why should they go through life without their big brother? I wish this man had been badly hurt in the accident so at least he'd be reminded of it every day of his life. I used to believe in God and go to church but I can't face it any more. Everyone expects me to have got over it.

What can I do?

Yours
Catherine

BACK DOWN THE MOUNTAIN

AIM: to consider how we will put Jesus words into practice

Jesus delivered this Sermon near the start of his ministry, and lived it for the rest of his life. The disciples who shared his life so closely could have seen any inconsistencies: there were none. As the series ends, the challenge we face is will we continue choosing to live this radically different kingdom lifestyle daily.

'Enter through the narrow gate. For wide is the gate and broad is the road that leads to destruction, and many enter through it. But small is the gate and narrow the road that leads to life, and only a few find it. Watch out for false prophets. They come to you in sheep's clothing, but inwardly they are ferocious wolves. By their fruit you will recognise them. Do people pick grapes from thornbushes, or figs from thistles? Likewise every good tree bears good fruit, but a bad tree bears bad fruit. A good tree cannot bear bad fruit, and a bad tree cannot bear good fruit. Every tree that does not bear good fruit is cut down and thrown into the fire. Thus, by their fruit, you will recognise them. Not everyone who says to me, "Lord, Lord", will enter the kingdom of heaven, but only he who does the will of my Father who is in heaven. Many will say to me on that day, "Lord, Lord, did we not prophesy in your name, and in your name drive out demons and perform many miracles?" Then I will tell them plainly "I never knew you. Away from me, you evildoers!"

Therefore everyone who hears these words of mine and puts them into practice is like a wise man who built his house on the rock. The rain came down, the streams rose, and the winds blew and beat against that house, yet it did not fall, because it had its foundations on the rock. But everyone who hears these words of mine and does not put them into practice is like a foolish man who built his house on sand. The rain came down, the streams rose, and the winds blew and beat against that house, and it fell with a great crash.'

When Jesus had finished saying these things, the crowds were amazed at his teaching, because he taught as one who had authority, and not as their teachers of the law.

Matthew 7:13-29

TO SET THE SCENE

Make a list of the opportunities, decisions and challenges that people will face in the next six months. What have they got to look forward to, and what are they dreading? What might be a source of concern and what might be a source of blessing?

READ MATTHEW 7:13-29

1 Verses 13-14: list the differences between the two gates.

WHAT DOES SEARCH **THE BIBLE SAY?** **2** Jesus is not talking about entering the kingdom of heaven in terms of becoming a Christian, but is talking about entering into the fullness of life that the kingdom offers now. Look at these verses to find out what else is required of those who would enter the kingdom: Matthew 5:3-10; 5:19-20; 7:21; 18:3; 19:14; 19:23; 21:31; 25:34.

Whether we enter into the fullness of the kingdom is not a once-in-a-lifetime choice that we make, but an on-going commitment to making wise decisions on a daily basis.

3 Verses 15-23: last week we talked about not being wrongly judgmental. Here Jesus talks about the need to exercise good judgement in discerning false prophets. He calls them wolves in sheep's clothing – how might they be disguised today?

4 We are to recognise them by their fruits – what does that mean in practice?

5 What would we usually think of those who prophesy, do miracles and cast out demons in the name of the Lord?

Why does Jesus say he never knew them?

6 Verses 24-27: how might the wise man and the foolish man have approached the tasks of building their houses differently?

How do the wise man's efforts resemble putting Jesus' words into practice?

HOW DOES THIS

APPLY TO ME
7 What storms have you had to face in your life? Have there been times when you have been glad of firm foundations? Or have you faced situations that have exposed the fact that your foundations weren't as solidly on rock as you thought?

HOW DOES THIS

APPLY TO ME
8 Jesus commends those who put his words into practice. As you go back down the mountain, having spent some time focusing on these rich words of Jesus, what impact will this time have on your life? Open the letters that you wrote in the first session.

Talk about any answers to prayer, or any questions that remain unanswered. Did this series meet your expectations? What words of Jesus have had the most impact on you?

9 How can you encourage one another to keep entering into the fullness of the kingdom of heaven, and to put into the practice the words of Jesus? What could you do in the coming weeks and months that will remind you corporately of what you have studied here?

WORSHIP

The Verve sang that life was a 'bittersweet symphony'. Whatever the future holds for us, we know that there will be good times and bad, successes and failures, times of feeling close to God and times when he seems distant, the bitter and the sweet. This worship time will give everyone a brief opportunity to commit themselves to life in the kingdom, whatever it might look like.

Look again at the sheet of future opportunities and challenges that you compiled at the start of this session. Have some slices of lemon and a dish of honey with some breadsticks. Invite people to eat the honey, thanking God for his presence in their lives now and in the future, and the blessings that are to come.

Eat some lemon, recognising that God will be with us even in the difficult times. Ask God to give you the strength to face the challenges, the wisdom to choose foundations that will stand the storm, and the knowledge of his presence throughout.

Pray for one another, about the future events on the sheet, and for kingdom fruitfulness.

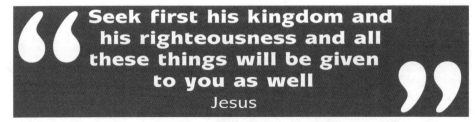

> **Seek first his kingdom and his righteousness and all these things will be given to you as well**
>
> Jesus

SESSION 8

LEADERS' GUIDE

TO HELP YOU LEAD

You may have led a housegroup many times before; this may be your first time. Here is some advice on how to lead these studies.

- As the group leader, you don't have to be an expert or a lecturer. You are there to facilitate the learning of the group members – helping them to discover for themselves the wisdom in God's word. You should not be doing most of the talking or dishing out the answers, whatever the group expects from you!

- You do need to be aware of the group's dynamics, however. People can be quite quick to label themselves and each other in a group situation. One person might be seen as the expert, another the moaner who always has something to complain about. One person may be labelled as quiet and not expected to contribute, another person may always jump in with something to say. Be aware of the different types of individuals in the group, but don't allow the labels to stick. You may need to encourage those who find it hard to get a word in, and quieten down those who always have something to say. Talk to members in between sessions to find out how they feel about the group.

- The sessions are planned to try and engage every member in actively learning. Of course you can't force anyone to take part if they don't want to, but it won't be too easy to be a spectator. Activities that ask everyone to write down a word, or to talk in twos, and then report back to the group are there for a reason. They give everyone space to think and form their opinion, even if not everyone voices it out loud.

- Do adapt the sessions for your group as you feel is appropriate. Some groups may know each other very well and will be prepared to talk at a deep level. New groups may need a bit of time to get to know each other before making themselves vulnerable, but encourage members to share their lives with each other.

- Encourage a number of replies to each question. The study is not about finding a single right answer, but about sharing experiences and thoughts in order to find out how to apply the Bible to people's lives. When brainstorming, don't be too quick to evaluate the contributions. Write everything down and then have a look to see which suggestions are worth keeping.

- Similarly encourage everyone to ask questions, to voice doubts and to discuss difficult issues. Some parts of the Bible are difficult to understand. Sometimes the Christian faith throws up paradoxes. Painful things happen to us that make it difficult to see what God is doing. A housegroup should be a safe place to express all of this. If discussion doesn't resolve the issue, send everyone away to pray about it in between sessions and ask your minister for advice!

• Give yourself time in the week to read through the Bible passage and the questions. Read the leaders' notes for the session, as different ways of presenting the questions are sometimes suggested. However, during the session, don't be too quick to come in with the answer – sometimes we need space to think.

• Delegate as much as you like! The easiest activities to delegate are reading the text, and the worship suggestions, but there are other ways to involve group members. Giving people responsibility can help them own the session much more.

• Pray for group members by name, that God would meet with them during the week. Pray for the group session, for a constructive and helpful time. Ask the Lord to equip you as you lead the group.

THE STRUCTURE OF EACH SESSION

Feedback: find out what people remember from the previous session, or if they have been able to act during the week on what was discussed last time.

To set the scene: an activity or question to get everyone thinking about the subject to be studied.

Bible reading: it's important to actually read the passage you are studying during the session. Ask someone to prepare this in advance or go round the group reading a verse or two each. Don't assume everyone will be happy to read out loud.

Questions and activities: adapt these as appropriate to your group. Some groups may enjoy a more activity-based approach, some may prefer to just discuss the questions. Try out some new things!

Worship: suggestions for creative worship and prayer are included, which give everyone an opportunity to respond to God, largely individually. Use these alongside singing or other group expressions of worship. Add in a prayer time with opportunities to pray for group members and their families and friends.

For next week: this gives a specific task to do during the week, helping people to continue to think about or apply what they have learned.

WHAT YOU NEED

A list of materials that are needed is printed at the start of each session in this Leaders' guide. In addition you will probably need:

Bibles: the Bible passage is printed in the book so that all the members can work from the same version. It will be useful to have other Bibles available, or ask everyone to bring their own, so that other passages can be referred to. You definitely need Bibles for sessions 1 and 8.

Paper and pens: for people who need more space than is in the book!

Flip Chart: it is helpful to write down people's comments during a brainstorming session, so that none of the suggestions are lost. There may not be space for a proper flip chart in the average lounge, and having one may make it feel too much like a business meeting or lecture. Try getting someone to write on a big sheet of paper on the floor or coffee table, and then stick this up on a wall with blu-tack.

GROUND RULES

How do people know what is expected of them in a housegroup situation? Is it ever discussed, or do we just pick up cues from each other? You may find it helpful to discuss some ground rules for the housegroup at the start of this course, even if your group has been going a long time. This also gives you an opportunity to talk about how you, as the leader, see the group. Ask everyone to think about what they want to get out of the course. How do they want the group to work? What values do they want to be part of the group's experience; honesty, respect, confidentiality? How do they want their contributions to be treated? You could ask everyone to write down three ground rules on slips of paper and put them in a bowl. Pass the bowl round the group. Each person takes out a rule and reads it, and someone collates a list. Discuss the ground rules that have been suggested and come up with a top five. This method enables everyone to contribute fairly anonymously. Alternatively, if your group are all quite vocal, have a straight discussion about it!

ICONS

 The aim of the session

 Engaging with the world

 Investigate what else the Bible says

 How does this apply to me?

A fuller version of these notes for leaders can be downloaded from the Spring Harvest website free of charge. For further details visit www.springharvest.org/workbooks.

NB not all questions in each session are covered, some are self-explanatory.

SESSION 1

MATERIALS NEEDED
• Bible, paper, and pens

• Notepaper and envelopes

TO SET THE SCENE As well as helping people get to know each other, this causes us to consider how we live. Is there an intentional choice behind the way we spend our money and bring up our children? The Sermon will challenge us, so we start by thinking how the course of our lives was set.

1 Ask someone to prepare this reading in advance. Find out how the different verses have had an impact. Note what people find challenging, so that you know what to emphasise.

2 Again, this is a good 'get to know you' activity with deeper implications. Encourage people to appreciate their diversity. Give them permission to be different!

3 Kingdoms have: a king – a ruler; citizens; boundaries; rules/way of life; a location; relationships between citizens and between the king and citizens; obligations – citizens to king and king to citizens; expectations; loyalty; identity.

4 The terms 'kingdom of heaven' and 'kingdom of God' are interchangeable. Matthew tends to use kingdom of heaven; writing for a Jewish audience, he would avoid using the expression 'of God'.

5 Perhaps the church has missed out on teaching about the kingdom of heaven partly because it is hard to grasp, especially the 'now' and 'not yet'. The kingdom is near, is upon you and to come: all of those things at once! We can experience the rule of God here, and the richness of relationship with him if we choose to, but we still look forward to the kingdom coming in all its fullness. Trying to explain it to a youth group member is not meant to be patronising, but a way of expressing a complex truth to someone who is beginning to think abstractly.

6 We are called to be different from: the Pharisees – the legalistic, holier-than-thou religious people; the pagans – those that don't know Christ; and the hypocritical fellow Christians for whom appearances matter more than their relationship with God.

7 Be aware the Sermon addresses a range of issues: character, evangelism – being salt and light, legalism and righteousness, murder and anger, adultery, divorce, swearing oaths, revenge, relationships, giving, praying, forgiveness, fasting, ambition, attitudes to money and possessions, trusting God, judging others, hypocrisy, relationship with God, entering the kingdom, fruitfulness and the foundations of life.

9 The 'spiritual' areas have tended to be things like prayer, reading the Bible, going to church; worldly areas are everything else! The sacred/secular divide is very pervasive, and can catch us unawares.

10 This might be an appropriate exercise to get everyone to do at home. The aim is not to encourage people to be smug and self-righteous, but to think honestly 'How much do I allow God to rule in this area of my life?'

WORSHIP Play some suitable worship songs or background music as everyone writes. They should seal their envelopes, and could hand them to the leader to look after during the series. We shall return to them in the last session.

SESSION 2

MATERIALS NEEDED
• Bible, paper and pens

• A variety of publications for 'Set the scene', tabloid newspaper, broadsheet, celebrity magazine, TV listings guide, men's and women's magazines

• A clip from a soap opera if using that option in the case study

• Large piece of paper and counters for question 10

IN THIS SESSION One of the activities in this session is to think through what the Beatitudes look like in practice. You can either do this by working through questions 3 to 8, or by considering a case study.

TO SET THE SCENE Don't let this go on too long! Looking at magazines can be a useful stimulus, but the danger is that we get side-tracked. Set a time limit. Ask for feedback on what individuals noticed during the week.

3 You could split the group into three and ask them to consider one of these Beatitudes each.

Poor in spirit: this is not about having a bad self-image. The tax collector recognises that he is a sinner. The poor in spirit are those who acknowledge they are spiritually empty and need God.

Mourn: this is about mourning over our sinfulness and that of the world, not about death. When Peter realised what he had done, he wept bitterly.

Meek: Jesus chose to wash his disciples' feet, displaying gentleness and submission. Meekness is rarely valued in our society.

The promise part of the verse should not be seen as the reward or the result of the first half. We don't receive the kingdom of heaven because we're poor in spirit. Jesus is the connection in each verse – he is the one who has opened the kingdom to those who are poor in spirit.

4 Lack of food and water makes us hungry and thirsty! Draw out the fact that a true hunger and thirst for righteousness might only come from going through difficult situations.

5 To show mercy is to be compassionate to someone who is in your power. Jesus talks about this same principle working in relation to forgiveness (Matthew 6:14,15), not judging and giving (Luke 6:37,38).

6 You would expect someone who was pure in heart to have pure actions, motives, words and so on – the purity would spread outward! God makes us pure in heart, (e.g. Ephesians 1:4), but we also need to keep ourselves pure (e.g. Colossians 3:5–10).

7 A peacekeeper wants calm, but doesn't address the underlying reason for disagreements. They might send the children to their bedrooms, and so restore peace to the lounge. A peacemaker will try to resolve any disagreements, and address the reasons why there is conflict. They might talk to the children about the need to take turns. Remind parents that probably everyone follows the peacekeeping role at times in order to preserve their sanity!

8 Mostly we suffer little persecution in this country because of our faith, although the experience of some in your group may be different. Remember those in countries where believers are killed for their faith. Try to distinguish between being a smug, irritating Christian and a Beatitude Christian who is persecuted because of righteousness.

9 If appropriate, ask people to share the word they have written down. There needs to be a balance: without Christ living in us, no effort will give us a Beatitude character, but we must put ourselves in a place where the Spirit can work.

10 You could draw a continuum on a large piece of paper like this:

Completely   Totally
unrealistic   ⟵————————————————⟶   realistic

Give everyone Monopoly counters and ask them to put them in the place on the line that represents how they feel – and then to explain why. Although the wisdom of the world says you need to be tough to survive or that you should pursue happiness at all costs, the kingdom of God is upside-down. People may have quite conflicting emotions and thoughts in response to this question. Allow them space to voice these conflicts if they wish.

CASE STUDY Use your imaginations to fill in any gaps about Alison. This exercise is to think what the Beatitudes might look like lived out in practice, not about prescribing model behaviour. Note we cannot always make decisions based purely on our personal values. In situation b) Alison may feel compassion for the boy and want to give him a second chance, but she will need to follow school procedures. She could, however, review pastoral care in the school to see if the boy was given appropriate support, and ensure his case is handled justly.

SESSION 3

MATERIALS NEEDED
- Bible, paper, and pens
- Photos of groups
- Large sheets of paper and marker pens for the brainstorming
- Coloured pens to fill in the time sheet
- Salted snacks, a candle, nightlights, and background music for the worship

You could also have some visual aids for this session: a bowl of salt, a salt mill, a torch, candles, spotlight, fairy lights.

When Christians discuss church, there is the potential for things to get negative and personal! In considering the type of community that Jesus intended the church to be, the aim is not to criticise or be negative about our current churches, but to try and look for positive ways forward.

FEEDBACK Ask for examples of Beatitude characteristics that they noticed in the week.

TO SET THE SCENE Find some photos from magazines or your own collection of different groups – sports team, scout camp, church service, local café, community centre, parents outside school. Stuck for pictures? Write these categories on a large piece of paper and get everyone to imagine what they look like!

1 Worship, living a kingdom lifestyle, enjoying fellowship and witnessing in words and actions to those outside the church.

2 Salt is a preservative: authentic Christians can slow down and prevent the deterioration of a Godless society. It provides flavour – being distinctively Christian and culturally relevant. It's a sign of peace in the making of covenants – bringing peace and reconciliation. It makes roads safe, melting ice – thawing people's hearts by showing them God's love.

3 Both the similarities and the differences in metaphor can be enlightening. Salt is bitter if eaten on its own – is the church meant to leave a nasty taste? Too much salt is unhealthy – raising your blood pressure. Salt is corrosive – eating into metal.

But can these characteristics of salt that don't seem to fit the church tell us more about what the church should be like?!

4 Light is used to illuminate – a lighthouse is a symbol of safety, showing up danger.

Light enlivens, expressing life and energy. The followers of the King are called to bring light and colour to the world.

Light exposes, revealing what is in the darkness. The people of God need to show evil for what it is and reveal the light of God's truth.

Light reveals – our lifestyle should show what God is like, bringing him praise.

Most types of light can enrich our image of the church. See how many you can come up with.

5 See also John 9:5. Jesus calls himself the Light while he is in the world. What are the implications of us being given the title 'Light of the World'?

6 A city set on a hill is visible for miles around. It is a place of safety – the inhabitants can see anyone approaching who might attack. It acts as a beacon for travellers –and a haven for those in trouble.

7 The Old Testament is history – the story of God's intervention in the lives of people in former times. Matthew's gospel begins with the genealogy of Jesus – establishing his place in the story. Jesus is also the next instalment in God's dealings with humanity.

The Old Testament is also about God's promise. It is full of prophecy, looking ahead to a promised Messiah – fulfilled by Jesus.

The Old Testament contains the law – the way the people needed to behave in order to be right with God. Jesus fulfils the law by showing what it was about – a heart transformation instead of legalistic practice – and by being the only person to truly live it.

8 Many New Testament passages show that we're not made righteous by obeying the law (for example Romans 3:20-22; Romans 10:4; Galatians 2:16). Our righteousness should exceed that of the Pharisees by going deeper. It needs to be a righteousness that goes beyond our heads and is shown in our actions, coming from the heart. It starts from the cross. Our new birth makes us righteous: our love for God and his forgiveness enable us to stay righteous.

9 People may prefer to do the time sheet exercise at home. It can be quite threatening to be asked to justify how you use your time when you may feel very busy. Point out that this is a self-audit. However, it can help to discuss these issues with others facing the same pressures.

SESSION 4

MATERIALS NEEDED
• Bible, paper, and pens
• For the worship, bowls of warm water, soap, towels, hand cream and seaside rock

FEEDBACK Ask everyone to share their 'salty' experiences from the week.

TO SET THE SCENE The discussion is about the law in this country and how we may sometimes disregard, or justify breaking, those rules that we think are trivial or inconvenient. You will probably agree with Jesus' teaching – that the law is necessary but can't make us good. What we need is a change of heart.

1 They all begin 'You have heard it said…' and then Jesus says 'But I tell you…', explaining how the kingdom lifestyle goes beyond keeping the law. Jesus is not criticising the law, but the Pharisees' interpretation of it and their pedantry.

2 Anger is not wrong; there is a place for righteous anger. God himself gets angry (e.g. Isaiah 30:27). We are right to feel angry about racism, sexual abuse and the huge gulf between rich and poor. Our lack of anger is a failure to care. Paul says 'In your anger do not sin' (Ephesians 4:26). The situation Jesus describes starts with a thought. This is spoken out as an insult, designed to inflame.

3 These situations were insulting, unfair ones, rather than physical assault or the threat of injury. If you were struck on the right cheek by a right-handed person, they would be giving you a backhanded blow which was considered a great insult.

4 Some of the signs of corrupted sexuality are: pornography, promiscuity; sex outside marriage; the portrayal of sex in most films – separated from its consequences; the rise in sexually transmitted infections; prudishness and embarrassment about sex – and so on. A right attitude towards sexuality will encompass self-awareness – being aware of our weaknesses; respect for each other; commitment to purity; respect for and celebration of marriage and so on.

5 Lust can be very addictive, devaluing those we lust after and reducing them to objects. Do not take Jesus' words about gouging out eyes literally, otherwise who would have two eyes left? We need to be self-aware, knowing what causes us to sin.

6 In a short study, it is very difficult to go into such a sensitive subject in depth. You will know how the issue of marriage breakdown and divorce have impacted your group. Ask them if they wish to look at this again at a later date. Jesus stands between the extreme liberalism of an easy divorce culture and the extreme harshness of a church that forbids divorce and remarriage.

7 People may speak from their own experience here. Stress the need for grace, compassion and to set a good example. Be aware that there may be some in your group who feel they have been badly treated by the church.

8 Jesus is not really talking about bad language, but about using places or things to give weight to what we're saying. That should be unnecessary for Christians: God is already in our transactions.

9 The aim of this exercise is not to come up with a model 'Christian' response, but to wrestle with difficult issues and be honest about putting these words into practice. We don't need to prove that we're perfect – but are we living in a 'kingdom direction'?

10 Whenever we talk about how to behave as Christians, we need to ensure we don't slip into legalism or 'salvation by works.'

Some of the reasons we should live rightly are:

• out of gratitude and love for God

• because God is holy and perfect and we want to be like him

• because Jesus did

• because it will be a sign of the kingdom to those around us (Matthew 5:16)

WORSHIP Get a neutral non-perfumed hand-cream, but if the men really don't want to use it they don't have to!

SESSION 5

This is a rich passage. Some of the ideas, such as forgiveness, will be referred to in future weeks alongside other verses in the Sermon.

MATERIALS NEEDED
• Bible, paper, and pens

• Slips of paper and a bowl

• A simple pendulum

• Oranges

FEEDBACK Has anyone has brought cuttings of individuals who speak with integrity? Was anyone more careful about their speech during the week?

TO SET THE SCENE Get everyone to write two activities on pieces of paper, putting them in a bowl. This is a good exercise in getting to know each other, but it does also have a point! Jesus says 'when you give, pray, fast...' not 'if'. We need to have an up-to-date testimony of our relationship with him. If they were asked 'when did you last fast?' for example, would it be recent? You can make this link here or in question one.

1 He says 'when you give/pray/fast.... Don't be like the hypocrites...they have received their reward in full....Your Father who sees what is done in secret will reward you.'

Giving, praying and fasting are obviously not to be optional extras, but a normal part of life.

2 Although prayer and worship in community are important, we must also develop our relationship with God, falling more in love with him, spending time alone with him. That strength of relationship will then enhance the life of the church.

3 One definition is 'pursuit of friendship with God.' It encompasses both the aim of our Christian life – to become more like Jesus (Romans 8:29) – and the means. Our spirituality is to be secret, not superficial or done to impress and to have an eternal reward.

4 Too much emphasis on experience, which is not Bible based, can lead to a vague mysticism, or an 'anything goes' spirituality. Focusing too much on doctrine can produce believers who know all the right things, but have no developing relationship with God.

5 Set up a pendulum – get someone to hold a weight on a piece of string. One side of the room represents 'truth about God', the other 'friendship with God'. Group members can hold the pendulum at the point that represents them, and set it swinging in the other direction if appropriate.

6 Get people to write a reason on a slip of paper and put it in the bowl. In turns, draw one out, and imagine how the person who wrote it might justify this reason. Other members can respond and encourage you to give. Remember we don't just have to give money.

7 This teaching on prayer, giving and fasting is intertwined with and inseparable from the rest of the Sermon which addresses such things as materialism, forgiveness, worry, adultery, integrity. Prayer needs to mix in with everyday life, not be a separate, pious activity.

8 Some ideas: TV, alcohol, coffee, soap operas, the Internet...

9 Draw out some of the rich ideas in the prayer: calling God Father; the coming of the kingdom; praying that God's will be done; God's provision; forgiveness; God's protection.

10 There is no contradiction as long as we understand that the reward is not salvation, it is something extra. It can be God's delight in us, a greater spiritual well-being, not material gain.

SESSION 6

Have a vase of beautiful flowers as a visual aid for discussing verse 28 later.

MATERIALS NEEDED
- Bible, paper, and pens
- Flowers
- Adverts from magazines, or videoed from the TV
- Piece of rope or thick string
- Red, orange and green coloured squares
- Coins for worship meditation

FEEDBACK Ask if anyone wants to talk about their diaries, but respect their right to secrecy!

TO SET THE SCENE Adverts seem to be everywhere – on petrol pump handles, on the back of till rolls, on the petrol station forecourt. They constantly tell us that we 'need' new things. How immune are we?

1 Jesus is against accumulating much more than we need (see the Parable of the Rich Fool: Luke 12:13–21), being selfish and greedy and valuing temporary things. It is not wrong to be a wealthy Christian, but it is difficult.

2 Shopping can be a regular weekend activity whether or not we buy: often done on Sundays; shopping centres or malls are 'temples' of consumerism – existing only for buying and selling; people look to products for meaning and identity.

3 This is not about earning salvation, but investing in things that will last, both in terms of 'good works' that will live on after us, and in our relationship with God. It is also about focusing on the kingdom of God, rather than accumulating wealth.

4 Encourage honesty! We all know the right answer. Find out if anyone has been burgled and how it felt. We would probably miss irreplaceable things, but shouldn't dismiss the sense of home and rootedness that our possessions can give us.

5 Give someone a piece of rope or thick string. As each worry is mentioned, tie a knot in it. This is a visual reminder of how restricting worry can be. Is it possible not to worry? How do we cope with worry?

6 Having a sense of priorities – life is more important than food (verse 25, 33). Trusting in our Father to provide for us (verse 26, 30, 32). Realising our value in God's sight (verse 26). Realising the futility of worry and the wasted energy that goes into it (verse 27). Appreciating the richness and beauty of God's creation and provision (verse 29). Direct everyone to look at the flowers if they haven't noticed them!

7 Go through the prayer phrase by phrase, thinking about how it provides an antidote to worry.

8 The aim of this activity is to think about what we consider to be essential to life. There will probably be disagreements! Should we expect God to provide us with the bare minimum, or enable us to enjoy the riches of his creation? Does our money come from our employer or from God?

You could split the group into twos or threes to enable everyone to get involved in the discussion. Give each group three coloured squares – one red, one orange and one green.

After they have discussed this, read through the 'daily bread' list and ask them to hold up green for 'yes', red for 'no' and orange for 'maybe'. Then talk about the results. Similarly each group should come up with their three top tips, then feed back to the rest, collating the overall top three tips.

9 If your group are not familiar with the Queen Vic or the Royle family, think of other situations that are more appropriate. The aim is to communicate a very familiar Christian phrase to those outside the church – in doing so we may be helped to understand it better. Have a 'jargon monitor' who rings a bell every time someone slips into Christian jargon.

WORSHIP Provide everyone with a few coins. Ask someone to read the text slowly over some background music as a form of meditation, providing spaces to think and respond to God individually. Ask people to share anything they felt God said to them, and end by praying for each other.

SESSION 7

MATERIALS NEEDED
• Bible, paper, and pens

• Heavy rucksack

• Paper with human outline on – enough for two each

• Lots of paints, crayons, coloured pencils and felt pens

FEEDBACK Have a look at the adverts that have been brought along.

Ask someone to wear a heavy rucksack from the start of the session, to represent the weight and burden that unforgiveness can be. This will have more impact if they arrive wearing it, and keep it on all evening, when serving coffee and sitting down. Organise it in advance so no one else knows. A plank of wood and some sawdust could provide a visual aid for verse 5.

TO SET THE SCENE Be sensitive to those who may have suffered major injustices. Whilst practising the biblical imperative to forgive, we also need to remember the fallen world that we live in. 'Forgive and forget' may not always be possible. You may truly forgive someone but still remember what happened.

1 We will be judged according to the same criteria that we judge others. If we judge harshly, then we will be judged harshly.

2 State authorities have a God-given mandate to provide justice and therefore judgement (Romans 13:4). Parents have the responsibility to nurture and discipline their children, which requires judgement (Ephesians 6:4). Church leaders have a responsibility for church discipline (1 Corinthians 5:3). False teaching should be discerned (Galatians 1:8-9). We're called to judge whether someone is caught in sin (Galatians 6:1). Ask group members to look up these verses.

3 Self-righteousness comes from pride and arrogance. Believing that we're 'good' leads us to criticise those who don't come up to our impossibly high standards, making us blind to our own faults. True righteousness comes from God. Aware of our own weaknesses, we will point out inconsistencies in others with humility, first checking that we're right with God.

4 Verses 1 to 5 talk about how we respond to fellow Christians. Verse 6 shows the likely response if a hypocritical Christian tries to impose his standard of perfection on those outside the church.

5 Perhaps so that we will realise how costly forgiveness can be and so appreciate more the forgiveness that God offers to us. In order for God to forgive us, we need to be repentant and committed to change. In receiving God's mercy we need to be willing to extend that mercy to others. See Matthew 18:21-35. God asks no more of us than he will do himself.

6 Unforgiveness causes us to get stuck in our relationship with God because it blocks his forgiveness to us. Unforgiveness is contagious – it spreads quickly. It holds us in the past and can lead us to judge falsely. Unforgiveness weighs us down – this is the moment to talk about the rucksack and how it felt to wear it! Why do we carry round unforgiveness? Would we, if it was as visible as this rucksack?

7 There are lots of issues to be dealt with here. Again, the aim is not to provide a model answer, but to think through how you would approach this kind of situation. Split the group into twos and threes to discuss what advice they would want to pass on. Then feedback to the group.

8 Children can be selfish in their requests, but the fact that they look to us to provide shows the relationship they have with us. Parents in the group could share how they teach their children to have the right values. As children grow up, their requests can become more reasonable. They realise what their parents can deliver, and what constraints their parents may be under, and what they need to work towards themselves.

9 Feeling unheard by God can make us stop asking. These verses remind us of God's nature, of how good he is and how much he delights to bless his children. Unanswered prayer is not always easy to cope with. We have to submit to his sovereignty and choose to keep trusting.

10 This is similar to 'counting your blessings'! God has given us so much, even if some prayers go unanswered. Naming those things and hearing the stories of others can raise our faith.

WORSHIP This may be a new idea to some, but others who are used to being artistic will really appreciate the opportunity. Give it a go, and encourage everyone to try it. Give lots of space for everyone to think and pray. If they really struggle with using colours, they can write on the picture. No one should be pressurised into feeling different after the prayer if they need more time to forgive. Their second picture could represent their intent, or their hopes to be able to forgive.

SESSION 8

A big bowl of fruit would be a good stimulus for discussing verses 15-20.

MATERIALS NEEDED
- Bible, paper, and pens
- Letters from the first session
- Honey, breadsticks and slices of lemon

FEEDBACK Discuss the difference that forgiveness would make to situations that individuals came across during the week.

TO SET THE SCENE Write these on a large sheet of paper. During this session we will think about how the teaching we have studied over the last few weeks will make a difference to these situations. As we 'go back down the mountain', having listened to Jesus, what are we going to put into practice? This sheet of future events will be used again in the worship time.

1 The wide gate is easy to find, opens into a broad road, is attractive and leads to destruction. The small gate is hard to find, leads into a narrow road, is not used by many and leads to life.

2 Those who would enter the kingdom will:

• be poor in spirit, persecuted because of righteousness (5:3-10)

• have a righteousness that surpasses that of the Pharisees (5:20)

• do the will of the Father (7:21)

• be like children (18:3; 19:14)

• find it hard to get in if they are rich (19:23)

• not necessarily be considered respectable – tax collectors and prostitutes entering ahead of the Chief Priests! (21:31)

• have practically cared for those in need: fed the hungry, given drink to the thirsty, invited in the stranger, clothed the naked, looked after the sick and visited the prisoner (25:34)

How many of these categories do we fit into?

3 Verses 21 to 23 imply that outwardly they may look very spiritual, and not be easily discernible amongst other Christians.

4 We need to look at what they produce in character and conduct. What type of person are they when they are under stress, or when they think no-one is looking? Do they act with integrity and honesty? Do they liberate people or tie them up with guilt?

5 Usually these would seem like marks of someone who is blessed by God and doing his will! We need to look beyond the outwardly impressive things to behaviour in smaller matters. How do they deal with some of the issues in Matthew 5 for example – anger, sexuality, faithfulness in marriage? Jesus acknowledges those who do the will of his Father in heaven. This does raise the question of how they are able to do the wonders if Jesus never knew them!

6 Building foundations takes time. Presumably the wise man knew storms were likely, planned his house to last, dug foundations, and built something solid. The foolish man didn't think about bad weather, expected the sun to always shine and built quickly with less effort.

7 Encourage honesty and humility. Be sensitive to those who have really suffered and have no explanation for it. Bad things do happen to good people. The metaphor of the house is about deciding what principles will be foundational to your life, and gives no guarantee against suffering.

8 If questions remain unanswered, encourage everyone to think about what they want to do next.